All Families

Interfaith Families

by Connor Stratton

www.focusreaders.com

Copyright © 2025 by Focus Readers®, Mendota Heights, MN 55120. All rights reserved. No part of this book may be reproduced or utilized in any form or by any means without written permission from the publisher.

Focus Readers is distributed by North Star Editions:
sales@northstareditions.com | 888-417-0195

Produced for Focus Readers by Red Line Editorial.

Photographs ©: iStockphoto, cover, 1, 20–21, 25; Shutterstock Images, 4, 7, 8, 11, 13, 14, 16, 19, 22, 27, 29

Library of Congress Cataloging-in-Publication Data
Names: Stratton, Connor, author.
Title: Interfaith families / by Connor Stratton.
Description: Mendota Heights, MN: Focus Readers, [2025] | Series: All families | Includes index. | Audience: Grades 2-3
Identifiers: LCCN 2024025660 (print) | LCCN 2024025661 (ebook) | ISBN 9798889983910 (hardcover) | ISBN 9798889984191 (paperback) | ISBN 9798889984740 (pdf) | ISBN 9798889984474 (ebook)
Subjects: LCSH: Interfaith families--Juvenile literature.
Classification: LCC HQ1031 .S825 2025 (print) | LCC HQ1031 (ebook) | DDC 306.84/3--dc23/eng/20240701
LC record available at https://lccn.loc.gov/2024025660
LC ebook record available at https://lccn.loc.gov/2024025661

Printed in the United States of America
Mankato, MN
012025

About the Author

Connor Stratton writes and edits nonfiction children's books. He lives in Minnesota.

Table of Contents

CHAPTER 1
Easter and Ramadan 5

CHAPTER 2
Faiths All Around 9

CHAPTER 3
Strengths and Challenges 15

Interfaith and Mixed-Race 20

CHAPTER 4
Dealing with Challenges 23

Focus on Interfaith Families • 28
Glossary • 30
To Learn More • 31
Index • 32

Chapter 1

Easter and Ramadan

A girl wakes up excited. It's Easter Sunday. It's also Ramadan. Easter is a Christian holiday. Ramadan is a Muslim holiday. The girl's family celebrates both. Her dad is Christian. Her mom is Muslim.

Easter always happens in the spring.

The girl's cousins come over in the morning. They do an Easter egg hunt. They run around the yard. Each kid tries to find the most eggs.

After sunset, it's time for iftar. This dinner is a big part of Ramadan. People end their **fast**. They start the meal by eating dates.

Did You Know?

In 2022 and 2023, three major religious holidays overlapped. They were Easter, Ramadan, and Passover.

 During Ramadan, Muslims don't eat between sunrise and sunset.

For dessert, the girl enjoys a chocolate egg from Easter. She feels lucky to be part of an **interfaith** family.

Chapter 2

Faiths All Around

Religion is a major part of many people's lives. In North America, Christianity is the most common religion. Two in three Americans are Christian. Many Christians are Protestant. Others are Catholic.

Many Christians go to church on Sundays to celebrate their faith.

Judaism is another common faith. Islam is also popular. Other people practice Buddhism. Some follow Hinduism. The United States has many other religions, too.

Religion touches on key parts of life. It can guide people's values. It explains right and wrong. It shows ways to be good.

Did You Know?

Unitarian Universalism accepts multiple faiths. Bahá'í does, too.

 Muslims celebrate their faith in buildings called mosques.

Faith can also help answer hard questions. For example, what happens after people die? Religions provide different answers. Some religions believe in heaven. In others, people are born again on Earth.

Religions are important to many **cultures**. They help form communities. People gather at a place of worship. It may be a mosque, temple, or church. **Rituals** play a role there. Prayers are one type of ritual.

Some families are not religious. They may be **atheist**. Other families practice only one religion. And some families follow more than one. These families are known as interfaith families. In interfaith

 Some families have one parent who is religious and one parent who is not.

families, each parent follows a different religion. Parents may raise their kids to follow only one religion. Or the kids may follow both.

Chapter 3

Strengths and Challenges

Interfaith families can have many strengths. One is more choices. Children grow up with adults who believe different things. So, children learn about more than one religion.

 In some religions, people may learn another language.

 Celebrating differences can make people feel more connected.

At first, kids might practice both religions. Later, they may settle on one or the other. Or they may find a new religion. They may also decide they're not religious. This ability can feel freeing. It gives children power over their lives.

Being in an interfaith family can also help in the wider world. That's because people are diverse. They believe different things. Interfaith children are often more open to this variety. They accept different ways of looking at the world.

In the early 2020s, about one in four marriages were interfaith.

Kids in interfaith families face challenges, too. They can feel split between two **identities**. They might feel pulled in two directions. Children may not know what is right for them. Should they be more like one parent? Or should they follow the other parent?

Another challenge can come from outside the family. Some people don't understand interfaith families. So, they may ask children about their religion. It could be

 Kids in interfaith families may pray with just one parent.

classmates. Or it could be extended family members. People might ask how kids can follow more than one religion. These questions can feel confusing or painful.

MANY IDENTITIES

Interfaith and Mixed-Race

Many interfaith families are also **mixed-race**. Sometimes, these families are treated unfairly. That's because some people believe **stereotypes** about certain religions. Other stereotypes are based on skin color. People might act on those stereotypes. They treat others wrongly. They discriminate.

Kids may see their parents being treated badly. Other times, kids themselves might be treated badly. This can be painful. Talking about the experience can help. No child or family should be treated this way.

Mixed-race families are one of the fastest-growing groups in the United States.

Chapter 4

Dealing with Challenges

More children are in interfaith families than ever before. Even so, interfaith families are still a minority. Some kids don't know any other interfaith children. So, these kids might feel **isolated**.

It's okay to feel sad or confused. Talking about it with a trusted adult can often help.

23

If that happens, kids can talk to their parents about it. That can help kids feel less alone.

Faith communities can also be helpful. Communities are a powerful part of religion. They can give people a strong sense of belonging. Kids' extended families can help, too. They can help kids become more connected with their cultures.

Some interfaith families feel like they're part of two communities.

 In many religions, people have outdoor gatherings such as picnics and parties.

That can be a huge strength. But other interfaith families don't feel accepted by either community. That can be a big challenge. However, many cities have interfaith groups. These groups bring interfaith families and communities together.

Interfaith children may stand out. But often, they learn that difference is a strength. Differences can lead to new ways of seeing the world. That can help people solve hard problems.

Sometimes, classmates might be curious about kids who practice more than one religion. These

Did You Know?

Some parents let their children choose their own religion.

 It's important to show kindness when talking about religion.

children may ask questions. That way, they can try to learn what it's like. But they should always be respectful. Every family is different in its own way.

FOCUS ON
Interfaith Families

1. Write a paragraph explaining the main ideas of Chapter 3.

2. What do you think are some of the best parts of being in an interfaith family? Why?

3. What is the most common religion in the United States?
    - **A.** Christianity
    - **B.** Buddhism
    - **C.** Islam

4. How might being in an interfaith family help a kid deal with challenges?
    - **A.** An interfaith family is the most common type of family.
    - **B.** An interfaith family believes in only one right way to live.
    - **C.** An interfaith family already has differences.

5. What does **diverse** mean in this book?

*That's because people are **diverse**. They believe different things.*

    A. coming from small cities
    B. having many different kinds
    C. believing in the same things

6. What does **discriminate** mean in this book?

*People might act on those stereotypes. They treat others wrongly. They **discriminate**.*

    A. to stop an action after learning something new
    B. to believe something that is correct and true
    C. to treat someone unfairly based on a wrong idea

Answer key on page 32.

Glossary

atheist
Having no belief in a god or gods.

cultures
Groups of people and how they live, such as customs and beliefs.

fast
A period of time when people do not eat.

identities
The traits, labels, and beliefs that people use to define themselves.

interfaith
Having people of different religions together.

isolated
Set apart from the rest.

mixed-race
When a person is made up of two or more ethnic backgrounds.

rituals
Words or actions performed as part of a religion or culture.

stereotypes
Overly simple and harmful ideas of how all members of a certain group are.

To Learn More

BOOKS

Andrews, Elizabeth. *Islam*. Minneapolis: Abdo Publishing, 2024.

Foran, Racquel. *A Look at Hinduism*. San Diego: BrightPoint Press, 2024.

McClain, AnneMarie, and Lacey Hilliard. *Talking About Religion*. Ann Arbor, MI: Cherry Lake Publishing, 2023.

NOTE TO EDUCATORS

Visit **www.focusreaders.com** to find lesson plans, activities, links, and other resources related to this title.

Index

A
atheism, 12, 16

B
Buddhism, 10

C
choices, 15
Christianity, 5–7, 9
community, 12, 24–25

E
extended families, 19, 24

H
Hinduism, 10

I
identities, 18
Islam, 5–7, 10

J
Judaism, 6, 10

M
mixed-race families, 20

R
rituals, 12

S
stereotypes, 20

Answer Key: 1. Answers will vary; **2.** Answers will vary; **3.** A; **4.** C; **5.** B; **6.** C